I Am Lifted
A Journey to a Better Life

Denise Eaddy-Richardson

authorHOUSE®

AuthorHouse™
1663 Liberty Drive
Bloomington, IN 47403
www.authorhouse.com
Phone: 1-800-839-8640

© 2011 Denise Eaddy-Richardson. All rights reserved.

No part of this book may be reproduced, stored in a retrieval system, or transmitted by any means without the written permission of the author.

First published by AuthorHouse 2/21/2011

ISBN: 978-1-4520-6311-9 (e)
ISBN: 978-1-4520-6310-2 (hc)
ISBN: 978-1-4520-6309-6 (sc)

Library of Congress Control Number: 2010917077

Printed in the United States of America

Certain stock imagery © Thinkstock.

This book is printed on acid-free paper.

Because of the dynamic nature of the Internet, any Web addresses or links contained in this book may have changed since publication and may no longer be valid. The views expressed in this work are solely those of the author and do not necessarily reflect the views of the publisher, and the publisher hereby disclaims any responsibility for them.

I AM LIFTED

I am lifted above the everyday drudgery of life.
I am lifted above the smallness of vision.
I am lifted above the boundaries of separation.
I am lifted above being satisfied with little knowledge of God.
I am lifted above oppression, fear and guilt.
I am lifted above an ordinary life.
I am lifted above a babbling mind.
I am lifted above pain and pressure.
I am lifted above sadness and despair.
I am lifted into purpose.
I am lifted onto God's highway.
I am lifted by the Holy Spirit safely into the arms of God.

The Journey

Last summer I told my daughter of my desire to start a business. As I brainstormed for an idea to build a business around, my daughter said, "Why don't you open a business and be what you are?"

"What's that?" I wondered aloud.

"A life coach—you are the best life coach I know."

I looked at her with amazement. She amazes me continually because she is older than her years in wisdom. My life's purpose, as I understand it, has always been to help people. I am a certified teacher, guidance counselor and an attorney. I have worked in all of these capacities. All of my labor has been a labor of love. In each position, I have helped people move from one place in their lives to another. Now I am entering a new phase of my life and seeking to help people move their lives forward in a different way.

Just the thought of life coaching stirred something within me. It made my imagination soar and took me back to the passions of my youth—public speaking and writing. I have long felt that I wanted to write—no, that I was supposed to write a book. But now for the first time in decades, I actually thought about doing it. I want to use the book in conjunction with my coaching.

I immediately began to research information regarding life coaching. I took surveys and set up appointments to have a couple of coaching sessions of my own. I participated in tele-sessions and reviewed information for certification. I realized that I had to come to terms with myself before I could be an effective coach for others. With the goal in mind of inspiring others to live their best lives with power and abundance, I decided that it was time for me to begin living that way in all aspects of my life. So, I set out on a quest of reading and learning.

My lessons began with Iyanla Vanzant's *One Day My Soul Just Opened Up*. I could not follow her script and read designated portions each day. My soul was too thirsty. I read three or four passages each day. Sometimes I reread them before moving forward. I read, prayed, meditated and wrote. I grew.

My first attempts at meditation were calming but not revealing. I sat down in a quiet space and tried to cease my thought process. It was difficult because my mind races; I am always thinking. I have often reflected that my mind works like the computer programs which allow many screens to be open at the same time. Multi-tasking was a work created for me. It was difficult initially to abandon thought and just Be. I concentrated on the word "be" saying it over and over to myself. I spent at least fifteen minutes each morning and each night being still and learning to stifle thought. After two weeks of meditating, I settled down and went immediately into a quiet space. It was a place I had never been before.

My meditations drew me into a calmness that I had barely met before—I had known only fleeting sensations.

One day I settled myself down into what I believed would be a blissful calm meditation. Before I knew what was happening, I was ushered into a field of white light, electric energy. I felt as though the hairs on my head were standing on end. The energy began to pulsate through my body invigorating my limbs, my upper body and my mind. I was blown away. Then suddenly, I felt as though I was literally thrown out of my meditation. My energy level was sky high. Well-being coursed through my veins. I was more than happy—I was ecstatic. I felt plugged in. I was totally connected to God. I felt powerful. If I had seen a mountain that day, I am sure that I would have been able to move it.

My meditations grew more and more powerful. One day my meditation was so intense that I felt as though I was at the throne of God. I felt overwhelmed and unworthy. I immediately began to praise and give thanks like a conditioned babbler. A voice spoke to me, "I am here, be with me." I quieted my mind in an attempt to just BE with the Great I AM. "I am always here," He told me. "Seek me, I am here." I wanted to stay in that place and in that time forever.

My journey had begun in earnest. I had visited with God through the Holy Spirit in meditation. It was not in another world, nor in a church. The visitation was inside of me. I was not surprised by this. Instead, it seemed like an affirmation of something I have known all along. God is within everything and everyone He created. He has provided us with an altar within ourselves. He is always there. I learned that my failure to access Him is just that, my failure.

I am committed to daily meditations as I travel this

road. They vary in intensity. Sometimes it is easy to slip into that special place. At other times, I have to press my way into the place of peace. From time to time my mind becomes so occupied with the troubles of the world that peace seems to elude me. It is at those times that I must remind myself to accept the things that are, surrender to the moment and return to now. I have learned new strategies for dealing with pain, conflict and tension. First I look inward. It is at the point of meditation where true issues become apparent. When I examine my emotions surrounding those issues, I am able to realize solutions or to discern that there is really no problem.

>
> In the secret place, there is no thought.
> There are only peace, love and tremendous power.
> In this place transformation is possible
> and ultimately inevitable.

Sometimes when you are trying to get to a new place or go to a higher level, you feel some sort of cosmic resistance. That is how I feel now. I know that I am in transit because I do not feel exactly like myself. The assurance that I have had for many years that I am exactly where I should be, doing the work that I should be doing is waning. I feel as though I have one foot planted in my life as it has been and other foot lifted and moving toward a new direction. The 'cosmic' pushback makes it difficult for me to complete my step. So here I stand with uplifted leg and foot knowing that I cannot replant my foot into what has been. I know with equal certainty that I must plant my foot on new fertile soil.

There will be no turning back. Once the first foot is placed, the second will surely follow. My life will never be the same. It will be renewed, enriched, invigorated and it will not be my own. So, how is the next step to be taken? When will the resistance dissipate? The step will be taken on faith at the moment of God's command. He will dispel the resistance. I need only to commit to readiness. I am in His hands.

The Writing

I had long been instructed to write. My instructions have become more and more clear. I am instructed to write, I get that. But my meager thoughts and musings while somewhat interesting to me can have no real importance to others. I mean, really, what am I to write about? What message do I have? I have come to know that the message is not mine to give. The message of peace comes not from me, but from God. The message of joy—again, not mine, but God's. And who would ever presume to convey a message of love without paying tribute to the source and the totality of love, God? It is no wonder that as I search through my little mind with even more limited understanding that I find myself bereft of cogent and sustained thought that will lend itself to the publication of a book. Yet, I am instructed to write my book. It feels like a quandary although I do not question what I have been told to do. I need to write because I have been instructed to do so. I have also been assured that everything I need to know, I know. Everything I need to have I have. I know that direction will come. My biggest obstacles are isolating the subject or concrete topic and continuing to write until guidance comes. I know that I will be spiritually led. So I have committed myself to the obedience of writing each day. Whether sick or well, happy or sad, I will write by faith.

This book is not a novel. It is more of a dateless, semi-topical diary. It is an attempt to share my journey toward living my best life through spiritual development. It is my quest to enjoy communion with God and to live my destiny as He created it.

Revelations

(Amos 3:7) Surely, the Sovereign Lord does nothing without revealing his plan to his servants and prophets.

    I had a shattering revelation today. It was a frontal attack on my ego. This journey on which I have embarked is not about me. I realize that I had given my mind over to my worldly or ego-based thinking. I have lived a delusional life in thinking that I have been in control. It is humbling to realize that although I have prayed for a closer walk with God, have attended church services religiously and have taught the youth with passion (which is pleasing to God); I have formed barriers between God and me. These barriers are formed by my resistance to letting go and letting God.
    I have prayed with persistence for God to reveal the next steps in my life. I know that there is to be an unveiling, an empowering and a launching. I have implored him to show me the way and the destination. I now understand that I have been trying to fit his will into my ego-based formula of madness. I call it madness because I know full well that it is,

"In God that I move, live and have my being." *(Acts 17:28)*. I cannot order my steps. I cannot precipitate a result in the name of God when I am not spiritually ready to receive the anointing which brings the result into fruition. So, I have been instructed to continue my quest of heightened spirituality. I must learn to live in the moment, to live less in me and more in God. I am admonished to lean, fully lean, on God.

In time the plan will be revealed. If it is revealed a piece at a time as I travel along this way, I will take each step in the moment in which it is ordained, and I will praise God!

How do you suspend thought and totally rely on the guidance of the Holy Spirit? I am trying to learn. I do know this though: As you try to abandon the worldly mind, it uses its trump card against you. It fills you either with physical, emotional or material pain, which debilitates you and competes for your spiritual energy. It is a battle to be won.

I awakened from my sleep in the middle of the night to these thoughts:

I am not who I have always believed I am. I have spent so much time concentrating on the physical, mental, social emotional me that I have forgotten the spiritual me connected directly to God. When Paul was bitten by the venomous snake and he merely shook it off, it was in recognition of the fact that his spiritual connection with God transcended the physical. *(Acts 28:3)*. When Christ called Lazarus, he did not call to physical man, He called to the spirit to come forth. The body in obedience to the spirit answered. *(John 11:33-44)*. When the woman with the issue of blood touched Christ's garment, it was merely a symbolic reflection of her spirit touching that of Christ's whose spirit was in constant communication with God. She was made whole. *(Luke 8:40-48)*. My wholeness is in the spirit within me.

My spirit has no weakness and no flaws. It is full of strength and is purposeful. I have lived a lifetime defining myself in terms of the limitations of the physical me which is the least of me. I am in fact a spiritual being without boundaries and limitations. I am whole.

I feel as though I had another revelation last night. I came to understand the illusory nature of this life. The purpose of this life is to perfect the spirit for reconciliation with God. That is a spiritual principle which has nothing to do with anything we attain within the physical realm. So while we continue to focus on earthly demands, pleasures and doing those things that serve the "me" that we have created and the deposits of self-esteem invested therein, we neglect our true purpose and dissociate ourselves from the power of redeeming and reclaiming our places with God. Once we are able to reunite totally with God, we will have the ability to walk on water, defy the elements and demonstrate the majesty of God to others. It is at that point that we will be able to claim ourselves as full joint heirs with Christ and can abandon all the limitations which press us so sorely. We will then be laborers in the vineyard bringing forth the kingdom.

Thy kingdom come.

> If I am able to believe without wavering,
> to know with certainty,
> I will be able to create miracles
> in my life.

I have learned that God reveals information before it manifests itself in the physical. He gives vision into those things that are yet to come. The first knowledge that I came to have that I felt was sent by God was the knowledge that my father's death was eminent. I was sitting in church listening to my father explain the Sunday School lesson. As he stood there talking with his hands spread apart and emphasizing his speech, I saw him laid out in front of the pulpit in a wooden coffin with flowers atop and all around the altar. The second information I received that I believe came from God was the direction to remarry my husband. I was reassured that I need not worry about the issues of our first marriage. They had been resolved. There have been many other instances when I have been directed by the Spirit to an action or have been provided with information I needed to effectively render service. I can truly attest to the fact that the God reveals his plans in order to create readiness. He also provides direction in order to open doors of opportunity.

My Commitment

My life has never been what I would consider a wreck. That is not to say that I have not had my share of problems. I have. I have loved hard—too hard and lost hard. I have suffered through two divorces. I have had financial woes despite always having a better than average job. There was a time when I was at home with a new baby and no money. There should have been money, but somehow the check did not make it home. Yet, I have always, by the grace of God, been able to find that there is still 'meal in the barrel.' *(1King 17:9-16)*. My children have never known need or want. God has always provided a way for us, and I know that he always will. I do not worry about material things because God has blessed me to "consider the lilies." *(Luke 12:27)*. I know that he will always provide more.

God has blessed me and kept me. He has directed my path in times of danger and has spoken to my spirit preparing me for times of loss or change. Now he has whispered into my ear and told me to take a new direction. I am ushered into taking this spiritual journey which I shall share with others. (As you will note, this is not the path on which I intended to embark.) I readily admit that I do not know the way. I do know that God does. I will share my journey in hopes that I will bless others as I am being blessed. I hope to share the light as it is being shed upon me and shared with me. It is my hope that my readers will look at my book not as a roadmap, but as a testament that each of us can begin on our own journey to fulfillment. I hope to inspire confidence that a way has been provided for us to live our best lives. We are not stuck in the meaningless or the mediocre. We all have the potential to live our lives in fullness which exceeds our wildest imagination.

I will follow God along this new path in total confidence that he will reveal the way and that I will know him better. As I progress, I pray that I will be better able to perform his will. I shall also pray that the Lord will send laborers for the harvest, "for the harvest is plentiful and the laborers are few." *(Luke 10:2)*.

Lord, I commit myself to the harvest.
The rows are long and the vines plentiful.
Some are bent to the ground heavy with fruit.
Others stand unconcerned, branches barren.
Many stand lonely anticipating the sun
and the rain that will loosen their fruits.
They silently cry out to join the celebration.

What shall I do in those times in which I feel stuck or stagnant? Knowing that God has made provision and plan for my journey, how do I move along the path that has been prepared for me? Sometimes I feel ill-equipped for the journey. Yet, I know that all is in the hands of God. Where I am at this moment, is where I need to be to learn the lesson being taught. My worldly self has muddied the waters. My mental clarity has been compromised. Still I know that the confusion and stagnation I feel are mental illusions designed to halt my walk. The illusions cannot prosper because they have no basis in God. I therefore turn to the Holy Spirit seeking the light that She has placed within me. The Spirit tells me that I am well when I would otherwise submit to sickness. She tells me that I can when I cannot see how. She admonishes me that my walk is by faith and not by physical sight. I may never understand how, but I know that God's plan for me shall be accomplished. The movement that I must make is not of my own volition. It is of God's will. When I yield, He will provide me with vision and clarity for my walk of faith.

I will follow the example of Christ and be creative in my environment. I will create joy where there is sorrow (in all things give thanks), comfort where there is dis-ease, (cast your cares upon him), clarity in confusion (God does not dwell in confusion), hope in despair (come that you may have life more abundantly) plenty in want. I will reflect God within me. *(I Thess. 5:18; Psalm 55:22; I Cor. 14:33; John 10:10).*

On Meditation

One night I lay tossing and turning in my bed. There was a sharp throbbing pain in my side. Despite taking a pain pill, I could get no comfort. I fought with my covers and moaned for rest. Then it occurred to me: "You can stop this pain. Go inside yourself and heal yourself." I lay on my back and went into meditation. I could feel the Holy Presence. Through my mind I said, "I came to be healed, to stop the pain. I will leave it here." I left the pain. When I came out of my meditative state, I was at peace and empowered. I had no pain and have not experienced that sort of pain since.

When this miracle happened, my mind was certain of the outcome. I had complete and perfect faith that I could absolve myself of the pain through meditation. I knew in those moments that God had given me a power to exercise on my behalf. I know that there will be other moments of great power and vision.

The other night was rough. My head ached, hot flashes

I Am Lifted

rode through my body with labor-like timing. Every time I managed to drift into sleep, my husband would settle into a pattern of deep, loud snoring. Each time I awakened feeling startled and tortured. Then the bad dreams came. Reel after reel of distorted, confused and disjointed images played themselves on the screen of my mind in frightening, vivid color. I was exhausted, angry and in pain. I struggled to capture the renewal that I thought only sleep could provide. It was then that I heard my inner voice say, "You don't need sleep; you need peace. Seek it." I left my bed and went to a quiet place to meditate. It was not easy. Distorted images continued to run through my mind. Trying to suppress them was a struggle. I would push them down as I exhaled only to have them resurface as I inhaled. I kept seeking that place. I needed to get to the point of communion. Then through my desperation I heard a familiar voice, "I am here." Suddenly, I was at peace. I was able to rise above my thoughts. The dreams stopped. The headache ceased. I was enveloped by a wonderful, blessed peace.

In the course of my meditation I came to understand that I was involved in a self-imposed battle created by my ego-based mind to make me fearful and derail me from my course. If I had gotten frantic and caught up, I would have been thrown off the center that I have found. I would begin to forget the things I have learned: to live in the present, that all my needs have been provided for, pain can be healed, peace is mine for the seeking and God is always present within me. This battle had been won. There will surely be others.

Rising above thought requires patience and practice. You must relinquish yourself, your surroundings, your relationships, your concerns and enter into space. Bring nothing to that place for it is not yours to fill. Wait there. The Holy Spirit will enter in.

God is perfection. There is no flaw, no blemish, and no weakness in Him. Man was created by God who knows only perfection. How then did man become imperfect? Is the imperfection that he perceives within himself guilt and does he live in self-imposed punishment for disobedience? How else could God's creation become corrupted? Through our delusions of powerlessness and imperfection, we have created illness, famine and blight. If the maladies of the body and society are mental creations or illusion, how can they be dispelled? Each of us must awaken. The mirror of distortion must be exchanged for the mirror of truth.

Last night I dreamed I had an out of body experience. I say I dreamed, but truly I believe it was not a dream. My spiritual mind took flight from my body. It momentarily looked down on my sleeping body then ascended in search of day. I found my true self flying above clouds in a brilliant blue sky. The sun was a flaming ball of light. My flight then took me above pointed pine trees and into valleys green from the nourishment of the same sun. I found myself melting into the great expanse of the universe. I assumed my rightful position and was whole. Suddenly, my body was pierced by a pain. My flight was abruptly aborted as my ego-based mind reclaimed my body. The illusion vaulted itself over reality; I was back in the body.

One day I entered into my meditation after riding my bike and stretching out my muscles. All through the ride and through the cool down exercises, I felt a certain buzz vibration of energy. I settled into meditation quickly. I was guided through passages—no, more like phases or depths to an altar of tremendous power. It was so powerful that I could hardly breathe. I felt as though it was too much power for me alone. I brought forth the names of my family, my husband and my children both biological and spiritual. After I laid them on the altar, I came to understand that the power was for me to take in. (It was days ago and this is the first I have been able to write of it. I am reconnected to the energy each time I think of it.) The power of those moments was so overwhelming that I felt that I could not contain it. Feeling as though I would surely burst, tears began to stream from my eyes in acknowledgement of its purity and its source. God was with me.

My meditation this morning did not rise to the heights of other days. Yet, it was peaceful and instructive. Miracles are of God. Faith is the invitation to their manifestation. God always performs through perfect faith. I end many of my meditations with the old Baptist incantation, "May the sweet communion of the Holy Spirit rest, rule and abide with us now and forever more." This is the presence I seek to take into the world. I want my presence to be the presence of one who is in constant communion with the Holy Spirit. *A Course in Miracles* (p.46) teaches that, "Communion, not prayer, is the natural state [of the relationship between God and man] of those who know. God and his miracle are inseparable."

As I rode my bicycle this morning, I saw a deer bound across the road about twenty yards ahead of me. The road was shrouded by big oak and maple trees. The canopy they created invoked images of a cathedral in my mind. It was the holy cathedral in which all of God's creations acted in unison and in concert with each other. The trees protected my sun sensitive skin from the damaging, penetrating rays of the sun while letting in slivers of light to illuminate the spirit of the holy place. The leaves rustled in the wind creating the melody of a soothing nature song accompanying the birds as they chirped their solos. The deer and I were the lucky occupants of that holy place if only momentary in that space and time. I paused to give thanks to the Creator.

As I resumed my ride, I began to think that this is what it must be like to walk with God in the cool of the day in perfect communion.

Struggle

For better or worse, my world is as I created it.

My mind was restless as I tried to settle into my morning meditation. It took me to boots (what?), cars (why?), people (dead), people (alive), animals (huh?)—just anything to prevent me from connecting with the Holy Spirit and enjoying the blessed communion. I set my mental clock; there was not much time for meditation. I had tightly planned my day. At one point feeling the frustration of being unable to rise above thought and hearing the clock ticking in my ears, I decided to give up. It was then that I realized that my mind was playing a good game of detour with me and was about to win. So, I called my mind out. I am tired of the fear that you create in me that keeps me from my perfect union with God. I am tired of you telling me that I am sick and feeding my body with pain. I am tired of you limiting my life and keeping me from the greatness in God that HE has appointed for me. I am sick and tired of you creating pictures of scarcity in my life. I want the health that Christ wants me to have. I want the abundance that HE came to provide. I want the fullness of life that God made for me. As I railed against my ego, I could feel myself being drawn closer to the Holy Spirit. I was quiet. In the quiet, I came to the awareness that all of the things I want are mine. I need only to claim them. OH—OH—OH---OOOOOOH, what a thought! It is not just a thought, it is a reality.

I ended my meditation feeling strong and empowered and headed out for my bicycle ride. As I rode my bike, revelation after revelation came to me. I have surrendered so many pieces of my life to my mind. For example, I have surrendered my energy. For years, I have been living with low energy. A little voice within me has long signaled that there was an incongruence in my life. My energy level should have been greater. Ignoring the voice, I attributed the lack of energy to my disease of the moment, whichever one was more prominent at the time. Thyroidism, lupus—it did not matter. I also noted that there are times when my energy level is high—when I am working with people, teaching, counseling. What made the difference? I discovered that when I did purposeful work my energy and enthusiasm are so high that even my mind can not fool me.

Trying another tactic, my ego told me, "You must be powerful beyond measure."

My spirit was quick to respond and straighten me out, "God is powerful beyond measure.—Do not be afraid you have a journey to take."

I was then reminded of something a pastor told me after I had completed a six years of guardianship over my friend and former pastor. "Eye hath not seen, nor ear heard, neither have entered into the heart of man, the things that God hath prepared for them that love Him." *(1 Corinthians 2:9).*

I love Him. I am encouraged.

Once again I find myself embattled. The struggle is totally internal. My energy is low. I am harried by hot flash after hot flash. They drain my energy and enthusiasm. (They make me sick! Literally.) I am uneasy, anxious and in spiritual warfare. My body aches which is an indication that I am losing this skirmish. I am tired and feel disconnected from my goals. Writing is difficult. I am stymied in the development of my business.

I am struggling; yet, I know the solution. I know where the power to prevail lies. Somehow, at this moment, I feel myself unable to access it; nonetheless, I know I will access it. I am trying to learn the lesson in this low place. I remain steadfast in my conviction that nothing shall separate me from the love of God. *(Romans 8:35-39)*. I shall prevail. I am in God; God is in me. There is no failure—just growth and progression toward perfection.

I will not be discouraged when I feel as though forces push back against my vision and the progress I have made toward it. It is an experience I must have in order to deepen my commitment to access the power that God has given me. I rest assured that His plan is sure and it will be accomplished. I know that my perception is not His reality. I rely on God to demonstrate that I am free and exalted. Everything I need is right here, right now as long as I remain in contact with His voice.

The night season comes because we lack the diligence to maintain the light. Yet, the light is always there. We, however, in our deluded ponderings, focus on worldly things and draw the curtains of night close in around us as though it were a shroud. As we banish the thoughts of scarcity, jealousy and pride, the light rays of goodness and peace will once again shine upon us. As rays shine, the night will steal away. We will be able to discern our way once again.

I feel myself coming to a new place. I am not exactly "my old self." I am in search of my true self.

Oneness in Creation

We spend so much time serving the illusion that we are separate from each other that we fail to acknowledge our sameness in God. We were created by one Creator. God blew the same life-giving spirit and air into all of us. The air is life sustaining to our bodies; the Spirit is life sustaining to our souls. He created us from himself and infused himself into us. We are one with Him and with all of his creations. We possess the same divine DNA.

Why then do we speak of God as though he has chosen one of us over the other? Would a loving God create situations that would perpetually doom His creations to strife and condemn us to continually be at odds with each other? No, He would not. We are one in the Spirit. God has no respect of person. He loves, honors, respects and holds faith with all of his creations. What he has provided for one of us, he has provided for all: salvation, peace, joy and sight. His gifts to us are the same. Receipt of the gifts is determined by our readiness.

There exists a dichotomy in the human existence. There is the spiritual creation of God which is ageless and eternal. There is also the physical self that is time sensitive, mutable and subject to decay. The physical self operates in a man made world of conflict, guilt, pain, fear and sin. The spiritual self operates within the world that God created for us. That world is a place of peace, joy and contentment.

We have, somehow, convinced ourselves that what we see, where we walk, what we taste, touch and smell is all that there is. We have become estranged from the best part of ourselves. Yet, even the most deluded of us will from time to time touch our spiritual selves and know moments of joy and peace despite the fact we cannot identify the source. These moments are like beaconing lights calling us into further awareness. "Oh taste and see that the Lord is good; blessed is the man who takes refuge in him."*(Psalm 34:8)*. The call is spiritual. Once we experience the bliss of spiritual communion with God, through the Holy Spirit, we will understand the blessing of the enlightened association. Then God will indeed become our refuge. It is at this point that our walk will become less physical and more spiritual—more by faith than by sight.

Learning to be the light of the world is a laborious task. We readily accept the fact that as Disciples of Christ it is our charge to be that light. We can agree that the two greatest commandments are to love God with our mind, soul, body and strength and to love our neighbors as ourselves. *(Matthew 22:37-39)*. But who are our neighbors. What shall we risk for him? How far must we go to demonstrate this love? These are tough questions. Until we learn to love unequivocally, without regard to special relationships, our lights will be dull indeed!

"We are One in the Spirit, We are one in the Lord." Peter Scholte (1966).

We are all God's creation. We, therefore, are connected through eternity. To the extent that we are able to acknowledge these tenets, we will be able to live in harmony and peace. We will acknowledge that each of us is a part of the other without separation. Through history and social constructs we declare that we are races, classes, caste systems and have social distinctions. These things are mere illusions created by man to confuse the reality that we are, in fact, one. They are meaningless. They are contra to God's plan of reunion because they serve to separate us from each other. Our purpose is to be reconciled with each other. We were created through love, by love, and to love God and each other. We cannot stand alone in love. We cannot mistreat, ignore or otherwise abuse our brothers in love.

John Donne put it so well. "Each man's death diminishes me, for I am involved in mankind. Therefore, send not to know for whom the bell tolls. It tolls for thee."

Each person estranged from God diminishes me—for I am involved with God.

To whom is God's favor given? God's favor is given to every one, without respect of person, without recriminations and without judgment. The question is not whether or not God has extended favor to us, but whether or not we have accepted or embraced the favor that He has given. God is not fickle. He is constant and unchanging in His love. All of His children are important to Him and all are of equal importance. Favor, which we think of as unmerited grace, is available to every one. It is not the exclusive providence of a few.

That which God has ordained for me is for me. I do not have to fight others for it. Likewise, you do not have to fight for those things which are for you. Our lives are not competitions. We are to be interested in helping each other attain purpose. For if you do not succeed in purpose, I, along with you, will be diminished. Our lives are designed to be in divine order. In divine order there is cooperation, joy, support, power and creativity. There is no competition.

When I look at my brother, I see myself, a creation of God. I know that we share the original breath of life.

Jesus asked, "Who is my mother and who are my brothers....Whoever does the will of God." *(Matthew 12:48-50)*. This simple inquiry and subsequent answer gives us insight to relationships. While most of us will answer the question who are my mother and brother by pointing to those attached to us by bloodline, it suggests an answer that fails to acknowledge kinship through God. We are more than flesh and blood. We are most importantly spirits united with God. Once we are able to accept this unity, we set off on a journey of purpose—glorifying God and helping others to experience the wonderful reunion. Through our spiritual awakening our blinded eyes are given sight. We are then able to see that all who love God are our family.

The Earth as a living creation rails against the inhumanity of man.

The concept of self-esteem is given a position of prominence in our lives. Some believe that our actions and responses are predictable based on the level of self-esteem that we hold for ourselves. Self-esteem indicates the level of pride, confidence or respect that an individual holds in his own worth. The concept is based on the physical world. The degree of self-esteem one has is often derived from material acquisitions, social standing, connections to prominence, physical features or physical prowess.

Self-esteem is not a spiritual concept. If we esteem ourselves as being a part of God, we begin to understand that instead of looking to ourselves, we must look to the value we confer upon our relationship with God and our desire to perform His will to determine our worth. Our estimation of who we are is then based on our identity of whose we are. We understand that we cannot hold ourselves out as separate. Nor can we exalt ourselves over our brothers. As we follow Christ's admonition to love our neighbors as ourselves, we learn that there is no difference between us. We are one and the same. The illusion of *self*-esteem then vanishes.

Life's Lessons

Love and Kindness

Life has a way of teaching us lessons. While I was earning my undergrad degree, I worked as a desk clerk in a major hospital. I was the communication center of a medical unit. I interacted with doctors, nurses, custodial staff, aides, dieticians and other support systems, patients, their families and the general public. It was there that I learned a very poignant lesson: Kindness and humility are essential elements of service.

I called the patient equipment office pursuant to a doctor's order. Soon a black woman in her mid-fifties came to the unit. I had apparently forgotten all of my home training and abruptly said to her, "I need a bedside commode."

"Hello, how are you?" She responded.

"I am fine," I answered embarrassed.

"Yes," she began, "you are fine, and YOU don't NEED a bedside commode. Even if you did, I am not responsible for your needs. They don't even matter to me. If you want something from me, you should ask politely for it."

I, usually very articulate, stuttered and word fumbled all over myself. Why? I had been arrogant and rude. Working with the doctors and perhaps my pursuit of education had evoked a certain faux empowerment within me that translated itself as arrogance.

In one fell swoop, Sadie, who would later become one of my favorite people in the world, deflated me and helped me to understand that love, kindness and humility would always be the most important tools in my toolbox.

My Desire:

I seek to live my life in the demonstration of the Holy Spirit and in power. I am instructed to walk humbly and in power. Humility is expressed through the acknowledgement that I can do nothing of myself. It is also an affirmation that you and I are equally yoked with Him. When I see you, I must see myself. There is no difference between us. The power is a direct gift from God to be used in the furtherance of His kingdom.

Love Judges Not

We are given to judging our sisters (and brothers). As a woman, I am most acutely aware that women are particularly judgmental of each other.

When I was a ninth grader, I met a girl whom I immediately decided I did not like. There was nothing in particular about her that I could cite as a reason for my dislike. The only thing that I actually noted about her was that she was not athletic. Yet, I had friends who were not athletic and I was not bothered by the fact. It was just plain and simple: I did not like her. Every time she came into my presence, I taunted, teased and bullied her.

We were in the same gym class. She was careful never to be on my team. That fact always served to her detriment when we played dodge ball. She was always my first target. I took aim throwing the ball as hard as I could. Being that I was a farm girl, I had very well developed arms. I tortured her with deliberation from September until Easter.

I have no idea what the preacher's sermon was about that Easter Sunday; nonetheless, I will always remember that day and what was spoken to me. I came to understand that my actions had been unjust and I needed to atone for them. If I did not, I could no longer profess to be a Christian.

It took me a full week after Easter break to get close enough to the girl to extend my heartfelt apology. I had been so rotten to her that whenever she saw me coming, she went the other way. I actually had to solicit some of our mutual friends to help me gain an audience with her. It was humbling, but I apologized to her in front of our friends. I told her that she had never done anything to make me dislike her. The problem was mine, something I had invented in my head. I explained what I had learned at church and offered her my genuine friendship. Although she was still frightened of me and uncertain of my conversion, she told me that she would like to me my friend. Amazingly she forgave me.

We continue to be friends today. I am forever grateful for the lessons of love, humility, kindness and forgiveness that she taught me that day.

What I have learned:

Learning not to judge is like relearning to see and think while learning not to think. Sound confusing? You bet it is. It is learning to see things as they are without the editorial comments of good and or bad. It is learning to perceive the potentiality of the person, object or situation to teach and accepting it as it is. This does not mean that you cannot perceive that change is necessary, but acceptance must come before change.

Most of life's problems are things we invent in our heads. Guilt, shame, notions of sin, judgment, condemnation are self-imposed mental creations that overshadow our lives with fear. None of these things is of God. They are mere illusions.

What I learned:

Life gives back to you what you give it. If you give it hope, it will give you reasons to be hopeful. Give life peace and you will create peace in the world. Unleash fear into the world, and the dragons of fear will return to pursue you.

Love Judges Not

Recently a good friend of mine was going through a divorce. His wife, whom I loved also, had told me that she was divorcing him. I had no problem with the idea of the divorce because they had not gotten along for quite some time. The divorce proceedings got quite ugly. She filed injunctions keeping him away from the home, made various, what I felt to be, malicious character allegations against him and managed to levy his wages to the extent that he could not maintain himself. At the same time she entered an order that he continue to pay the mortgage on the marital home. When he showed me all of the orders and reported what had gone on in the court, proceedings I was hurt. The hurt feelings led to anger. I could not understand how someone could profess love so strongly and abandon that love for materiality with such a vengeance. Getting a divorce was one thing, I reasoned, but being downright vengeful was another. When he asked me to appear with him for a court hearing, I was happy to oblige. I had practiced in the court for years, and I arrived at the court before any of the litigants. I actually walked into the courthouse chatting with her attorney. When I saw my friend's spouse, and I greeted her with a frigid hello. There was no smile and no cordiality. I was not rude, but I was not nice.

I have reflected on this situation often because I was not in character. Somehow I had allowed my anger for her actions and my judgment of her throw me off base. I recently realized that the failure of love to which I responded in this circumstance was not her failure, but mine. The moment I judged her as loveless, I indicted myself.

(Matthew 18:15-17) instructs us that "if your brother has offended you go and talk to him alone. If he listens to you, you have gained your brother." I had failed to adhere to this teaching, appointed myself judge and jury and behaved badly. Had I been loving, I would have been able to reason with my friend and help her to understand my angst surrounding the issue. Perhaps she would have been able to help me to understand her motivations. Perhaps I could have helped her to understand that even in divorce there can be a spiritual reconciliation of the parties.

What I learned:

Each time I judge my brother, I indict myself. The lesson that needs to be learned is mine.

God seeks to bless the world through you. Observe his mercy and be merciful without regard to person or plight. Judgment has no place. Any time you spend in judgment of another is time that should be spent in introspection. That which you believe you see in your brother dwells in you. *(Matthew 7:1-4).*

So long as we cling to the notion of sin, we continue to erect barriers that separate us from our brothers. These barriers take the form of judgments. Even as we try to live our lives free from "sin" we cast judgment upon our brothers. Once we begin to concern ourselves with living within God's plan, our view of sin begins to shift and topple barriers. Acknowledging that we are all connected souls, created by a changeless God helps us to understand that our brothers are mirrors of our souls that enable us to view ourselves more clearly. "Sin" then loses its platform of judgment and condemnation. It also loses its power of separation. The notion of sin as it invades our mind and creates the mental apparatus of separation is more damaging to us than the "sin" itself.

Evil is not of God. God has no being outside of love. In his lost state, man created the notion of evil. It perpetuates his perception of separation from God and creates separation from his brothers. Evil is born of judgment and gives life to condemnation.

Take a moment today and allow yourself to rise above thought and enter the place of joy and peace.

Purpose

Your life is not your own. The relevance of your life is determined by the degree to which you commit and extend your love, your life, your faith and your resources to others. It is not about you. It is about charity. If you are unable to love others meaningfully, then you have failed your purpose.

Your purpose is your truth. By living it, you praise God.

Those things that God wants you to perform; he has placed in your heart the desire to perform. Those places that God wants you to go, he has placed within your being the roadmap to get there. All that you need to achieve your purpose is within you waiting for your alignment with God's plan. Once your will for your life is in synch with God's will for your life, all will be accomplished and purpose will be fulfilled.

The Lord has need of thee. There are many who believe that we have need of God, but God has no need of us. We fail to realize that each of us is a part of God's master plan. Each of us was born into purpose. Our purpose extends well beyond ourselves. It is aligned with God's plan that all of man be reconciled with Him.

You were made for greatness with the ability to touch and bless the souls of others. Your greatness may lie in your hands through the ability to give a soothing touch or convey acceptance. Or, your greatness may be on your shoulders—the ability to bear the burden and lighten the load for others. Your greatness may shine brightly through your smile and compassion that restores hope and gives peace by letting others know that God is in control. It might be your tongue and voice that encourages others and lifts their spirits. Your ability to teach, preach, sing, admonish and instruct may be the only thing that lies between guilt and salvation for someone. Your gift may lie in your fingers which pens the words, molds the clay, paints the picture, strokes the keys or pulls the strings. The product of your fingers may be the elevator that takes a soul to the next level. Your greatness may be in your mental acuity or discernment which allows you to create and enhance the lives of others. Feet that move quickly to the aid of others harbor greatness. Everyone's greatness, no matter how it is displayed leads others to salvation. If it does not, it is an illusion.

As I recognize my being as an integral part of God and Him as an integral part of me, I realize that not only am I connected to God, but I am also connected to my brother. Upon this realization, I take my place as a worker in the vineyard. My job is to help facilitate my brothers' connection with God. We must each work in the vineyard. While helping my brother secure his place in eternity, I secure mine. As he helps me, he secures his. Come, the Lord has need of us.

My spirit has a place in the universe. I am connected to all that God has made. Once my spirit gains dominance over my physical mind, I will be vaulted to a higher place. It is at that point that I will begin to fulfill those spiritual tasks set before me. All of those tasks will be accomplished because it is the will of God. His will, will be done.

If we are to walk in the power of Christ and access the life of power that he has ordained for each of us, we must disavow ourselves of the thought that we are who we think we are. In *Mark 8*, Jesus admonishes us to deny ourselves, take up the cross and follow him. In denying ourselves, we separate ourselves from the self that we see. We learn not to view ourselves as a mutable flesh and blood creature. Instead, we view ourselves as spiritual creations that change not. We are in God. God is in us. He designed us perfectly. We will exist with Him in eternity. Who we are really has no relationship to what we see in the mirror, where we live, whose child we are or what we wear.

Taking up the cross is surrendering to role of our purpose in the grand reconciliation. We recognize that we are simply workers in the vineyard whose primary function is to help our brothers see the light of salvation and embrace it as their own.

The life that we lose for the sake of the reconciliation is illusory, it never truly was. God is constant and unchanging. There is no loss in Him.

There is a place inside of us where nothing is impossible. Miracles can be performed. Our self-created images cannot enter in. We are in that space as God created us. We exist as light, truth and forgiveness there. We are holy. Our purpose is to take the light to others. As we perform our purpose, we will perform miracles.

Lord I pray that I will fully see that I am of you. I pray that I will see the power that you have invested in me. I pray to see the path that is mine to walk. I pray for the visions established by faith. For my walk is by faith and not by sight.

Love and Peace

To the extent that you are able to see yourself in your brother, you are able to love. No more—no less.

Know that you are free. Whom the son set free is free indeed. *(John 8:36)*. What then shall be done with this freedom that has been so graciously bestowed upon us by the light of the world? The source of the light is pure, unselfish, unconditional, unquantifiable love. Your freedom then is to love without reservation. The ability to love unconditionally is a rare gift. It vaults those who possess it to places of spiritual completion. There is no higher goal in life than to love. It is the true reflection of God.

God has created within each of us a heart for loving—not the superficial love of lust, but the heart for agape love, God's love. His love is always extended whether it is accepted or not. It never changes. God's love is constant and unwavering. It is neither disrupted nor disillusioned by our mistakes or inadequacies. His love continues and abides even through our temper tantrums of willfulness. He does not judge our failures. Instead, he uses them to usher us into higher learning and awareness. God does not demean or castigate us because we have erred. He loves us through our difficulty and always seeks to perfect our souls and draw us closer to him.

I want to love as God loves—unrestricted, unafraid, steadily, without reservation or hesitation.

There is an old hymn that says, "Blessed assurance Jesus is mine." (www.hymnsite.com). The assurance of the love of Jesus and God the Creator gives us vision and strength to negotiate our way through this maze of life. It compels us to seek the truth and look farther than our physical sight. The assurance of God's love convinces us that through God we can do all things. We never have to worry about His rejection, frustration, depletion or inconstancy. The blessed assurance transports and frees us from the burdens, guilts and clutches of the past and lands us solidly into now which is filled with magnificent potential. God's assurance teaches us that we can make of the moment whatever we want. He is ever present to grant our request. Thank you Lord!

We tend to think of miracles as something well apart from ourselves. Not so! We experience miracles every day. Love is a miracle. The possession of God's love is a miracle. To possess and give love that seeks for nothing and requires nothing is a miracle. It is miraculous because love readily extends itself. Yet, it is never depleted. When we extend love, our capacity to love is increased. No matter how much love is given, it is never depleted. It renews itself in the giving. Giving love generates the by-product of joy which enhances the donor. Likewise, it acts upon the recipient by changing his attitude and creating a new vision within him.

Love carries the day. To the extent that I am able to love my brother and recognize our likeness through forgiveness and charity, I am perfected. The recognition of God within my brother is my second highest responsibility. The first is to know God. For, to know God is to love Him.

Love has no part in these things—guilt, pain, estrangement, betrayal, judgment, condemnation, sin, punishment, fear and isolation. They are not of God.

I give you my love; yet, I am not diminished. Indeed I am made stronger. Love is like a boomerang. It goes out and returns. It is also like an arrow it pierces its mark. The end results of agape love are joy and peace.

Love is the full measure of God. After that, there is nothing.

We spend so much of our time in the acquisition of things. We toil to earn money to buy houses, cars, clothes, land, furniture and so many other things. Yet, what does the possession of material things profit us?

When my father was ill he asked me to take him for a drive. As we rode through the countryside, he told me, "I have acres of woods, but I won't be able to walk through them. I have fields for crops, but I won't be able to plant them. I have cars that I won't be able to drive, houses that I won't be able to live in and money I cannot spend." Some may review my father's words and look upon them as the anguish of a dying man. I look upon them as a father's gift to his daughter admonishing me to maintain priority for my life. Anything that must be left behind is without substance and real merit. It is what one takes with her that matters. Love knows no boundaries and abides wherever the Spirit is. Peace and joy prepare a home for us in the next world. The Holy Spirit is the wind which feeds the sails on the sea of transition. She guarantees safe passage.

I watched my father during his transition. He readily relinquished his attachment to material things. But, his big, loving heart maintained attachment to those he loved through this life and into the next. I can still feel that love—boundless and wonderful.

The companion of peace is understanding. They are never separate. For peace understands the meaninglessness of this world. Peace understands that God has made provision and there is no want. Peace understands that we are anchored in eternity. Peace understands that God's will is immutable and will be accomplished.

Visions

Luke *17:6* "If ye had faith as a grain or mustard seed, ye might as well say to this sycamore tree, be though plucked up by the root and be thou planted in the sea; and it shall obey you." Dream a dream, write a vision. Act in faith and it shall come to pass.

Our perception is our reality. We often spend time wishing and longing for things or circumstances. Then we spend even more time rationalizing the reasons why our hopes and dreams cannot be manifested in our lives. We lack the true vision, the work toward its attainment and the faith that can transform a wish into an accomplishment. If we were to interview people who were able to turn their dreams into reality, they would all tell us that they believed in the truth of the dream and knew, with absolute certainty, that it would come true. Despite disillusionment and daunting odds, they were convinced that if they kept pressing, the dream would be actualized. Another thing they will tell you is that it was darkest just before the dawning of the dream into reality.

We must have faith that God has a magnificent plan for each of us. Pray for the vision and the way. Work the vision. Know that it shall be accomplished even though we may not know how it will be done. God knows.

To the extent that we are able to transcend the physical and connect with the Holy Spirit, we will be able to see visions and dream dreams that are gifts from God. The gifts are not ours. They are to be shared with our brothers. They will shine as beams to lighten the way to God. We will be the messengers.

My spirit seeks to soar and Be and throw off the trappings of the world. I seek communication with the Holy Spirit and clarity of vision. Oh to have union of purpose with God, my soul rejoices at the thought of it!

Power

Power and purpose. Power is God's. Purpose is God.

Walk in power and humility. Do not hide and suppress your power.

Reconciliation

All that happens in this world is not suitable for the participation of those who love God.

The anointing will come when all has been made ready for faithful service. Bow down at the throne; surrender all encumbrances of the world. The anointing will come.

There is something within each of us that compels us to seek the vision and see the light. Some of us hear an unfamiliar murmur that directs us. Yet, we can neither understand nor fathom it. As we mature in our walk, the low murmur turns into a barely audible stream. Sometimes it is a powerful stream of silence.

God is in us.
He is seeking us.

I Am Lifted

We must avail ourselves to him.

God looks upon our meanderings with the eyes of an indulgent parent who has decided that for better or worse He will allow His child to have his way. Like the father in the story of the Prodigal Son *(Luke 15:11-24)*, He waits patiently with everything we need to restore us to our proper position with Him. He stands ready to bless us and seal our identity in and to Him. No matter what we do, or how far our wandering, God, who has stamped us with His imprimatur, knows that once we recognize ourselves as ourselves, we will quickly run home to Him. There, He stands ready to greet us.

God stands with outstretched arms waiting for us to enter His embrace. He waits in the fullness of his excellence for us to receive him. God provides a radiant mirror longing for us to look into it and see ourselves in oneness with him—reclaimed and whole.

I looked at trees today. They stood stark, bare and naked. As barren silhouettes they stood against a snowy landscape reaching into a foreboding sky. They stood silent amidst those in the world who would judge them as dead. Yet, within them God has placed everything necessary for their revival and resurrection to green, majestic splendor.

We, just as the trees, belong to God. He has placed within us everything that we need for revival, resurrection and the assumption of our rightful place with Him.

God has provided a venue for each of us to come to him. For me Jesus is the way. He provided the example for us to follow to come into enlightment. His example is one of submission to God's will for his life. He lived in meekness and lowliness. He was patient in his teaching. He reached out to all who would listen. He honored children and women. He showed no respect of person by way of education, money or gender. He was loving and genuine. Jesus made provisions for those who followed him. He performed miracles routinely. For me, Jesus provided a splendid example. He walked with God. Following in his footsteps, so shall I.

Holy Spirit

There is inside of each of us a place where the Holy Spirit abides. Go to her for she calls you. She has the answers to all the questions of your soul. Seek her wisdom. Seek her joy. Seek her peace. Dwell in her love. There is nothing she will withhold from you.

The Holy Spirit bathes my soul in the pool of completeness. I lack nothing.

When you come upon a problem in life, look inside to the altar of your heart for solution. There, the Holy Spirit will shine light of salvation. The light will give vision to discern the truth of the matter. She will connect you to the resources of the universe that has supply for every need and solution for every problem. Through vision you will know the answer when you see it. It will speak calmly to you. There will be no tension between you and it. The answer will be as natural to you as breathing, and it will be in divine order.

Happiness is laying your problem at the feet of the Jesus and saying, "Here you deal with it," and meaning it.

After I surrendered to quietness, the Holy Spirit washed my soul in peace, love and kindness.

The joy of my soul stirs up within me. My valleys are full. The Holy Spirit is at work.

The Holy Spirit will be my companion today. I will seek Her wisdom.

Being in the Spirit transcends the human condition. Fears, unhappiness and guilt dissipate—they cannot enter the place of the Holy Spirit. Connecting with the Holy Spirit provides a conduit through which all the power of the universe can be channeled to you. The power propels you into the creation of your destiny to bring those things and circumstances that were ordained for you before your birth into fruition.

In John 15:4 Jesus tells us to, "Abide in me, and I in you." Abiding in Christ is not a passive state. It is a wonderful interaction made possible by the connection of our spirit to the Holy Spirit which is connected to Christ. There is transference of love and joy from Christ to us and from us to Christ that surges constantly when we abide in Christ. This love creates a third party beneficiary relationship wherein we are required to transfer love to our brothers. For Christ commands us to love one another.

> Today I enjoyed serenity;
> I embraced everyone with love.
> I listened with love;
> I calmed with peace.
> My soul enjoyed the sweet communion
> of the Holy Spirit.

Today I will honor the Spirit within me by taking time not to think. I will listen.

Much of our direction in life depends upon our readiness. Unless we are forced, we do not change until our minds and spirits come together and prompt us to step out of our comfort zone and transform or move a little farther along our road of life. Two summers ago, I decided that meditation would be helpful for me. I tried and tried, but nothing happened. I felt no sense of calm, no peace, no joy. Six years ago I purchased Iyanla Vanzant's *One Day My Soul Just Opened Up*. I tried to read it on several different occasions. I just could not concentrate on it. Last summer I picked the book up and could not put it down. I had reached the point of mental and spiritual readiness. I began to meditate and experienced the bountiful fruits of the Holy Spirit. I experienced a profound sense of peace, joy and closeness with God.

In much the same way, we are able to access the gifts that God has provided for us. When we go to him in mental (our mind under control) and spiritual readiness, we are able to access the promise.

Be careful when you feel your spirit troubled. Realize that it is giving you a warning. Do not embrace the disconsolateness. Pray and seek guidance from your inner wisdom. The Holy Spirit will speak and minister to you. The true question will present itself and the answer will become clear. The negative energy will dissipate and your peace will be restored.

In the time of trouble, I will go to my secret place and wait. In the peace of that place the real issue will unveil itself, and the answer will be discerned.

"And the Lord God formed man from the dust...and breathed into his nostrils the breath of life and man became a living soul." *(Genesis 2:7)*. When we read this scripture we often think of the breath of life as relating to physical life. The breath within suggests the human respiration in which the flow of oxygen is directed to the body joined with the blood in order to sustain the mortal being. Without that breath, it is certain that man cannot live. Yet, the verse does not tell us that man became a living body. It clearly states that man became a living soul. The divine respiration of breath was then the infusion of the spirit into the body; hence, the soul came alive. Just as the rhythmic flow of oxygen is required to sustain the body, the rhythmic movement and coursing of the Holy Spirit sustains our souls. The breath of air we take can only sustain our bodies during time. The movement of the Holy Spirit within our souls traverses through time and transcends into eternity. Our living soul nourished by the Holy Spirit is of God and eternal.

Sometimes as I travel along this journey, I find myself in places of brilliant light and remarkable power. Other times I travel through valleys of stagnant darkness. It is in the valley that I seek revelation into myself from the Holy Spirit. At this point of my course, I know full well that the obstacles in my life such as emotional valleys are self-imposed. My questions then become: Why am I sabotaging myself? Of what am I fearful? What burden of guilt have I placed on my shoulders? When I call, the Holy Spirit always responds and sheds the light of truth. Knowing the truth, I undertake my task to dispel the illusions. This sounds simple, but it is not. It is a process.

When we are lead by our sense of self, our lives are jumbled-up messes. We are out of synch with our spiritual selves and experience constant under rumblings of tension and frustration. We can give no satisfactory explanation for our state of uneasiness. Yet, we need only to look inside ourselves to find the peace of God. The Holy Spirit will come in and endow us with a sense of peace that sponsors mental clarity through which we can take inventory of our lives. We will then be able to discern those things that are harmful to our peace and well-being. The Holy Spirit will also empower us to take action against them.

Prayer

> Much Prayer,
> Much Power.
> Little Prayer,
> Little Power.
>
> *The Reverend Frank Riddenbery*

We are reconciled to God through prayer. Prayer brings our mental, physical, emotional and spiritual selves into alignment. We go to God knowing that He is within us, seeking the ignition of the divine energy He has stored up for us. Prayer allows us to acknowledge God for who He is while we seek to make manifest the strength and resources that He has deposited within us. Through prayer we affirm our belief that God can and will do what He says. We further affirm that He has provided for our every need.

I Am Lifted

Quite often when we go to God in prayer, our prayers are like a grocery list of requests. We enter into our prayer closets and tell God what we want. We lift our voices to Him. Perhaps sometimes our better posture would be to ask to hear His voice. God knows our concerns.

My prayers rise on the strength of my faith. My faithlessness, my fear and my sense of unworthiness reduce my prayers to meaningless words without voice or power. They fall without reaching the ear of God.

Lord please touch my soul so that I may receive my sight.
Lord please touch my soul so that I may discern the way.
Lord please touch my soul so that I may show my brother the light.
Lord please touch my soul so that I may celebrate the peace and joy of reunion.

The Blessed Association

Blessed are the pure in heart for they shall see God. *(Matthew 5:8)*. The pure in heart are those whose motives and actions are driven by love. Accomplished at the art of love, they develop a special communion with God and interactions with the Holy Spirit. Their relationships with God and the Holy Spirit open their eyes to the extent that they can actually see God in themselves and everything around them. They truly understand that God is love that is richly expressed in the universe around us.

God has faith in you. You are his creation. Just as a mother will always continue to hold faith in her children despite all contrary evidence, God continues to hold faith in you. You, as God's creation are a part of God. He has established his will for your life. No matter how hard you struggle against it, inevitably, his will will be done.

I Am Lifted

> God loves you
> deeply
> and
> totally.
> That is the truth.
> There is no other.

We often hear of people attempting to re-invent themselves or create a new image for themselves. These concepts ignore the fact that we were created in the image and likeness of God *(Genesis 1:27)*. Like God, our true selves never change. We should therefore seek not to re-invent ourselves. Instead, we should seek to know our true selves for therein lies fulfillment and satisfaction.

> God is truth. There is nothing else.

I will lift my voice to utter his praises. My soul will proclaim his marvelous works. His greatness surges within me and gives me life.

When God created me, he poured himself into me.
He poured in love and the capacity to love.
I shall honor that by loving him, myself and all of his creation.
He poured in truth and the desire for knowledge.
I shall honor that by choosing to accept the revelations he has for me and seek knowledge of Him.

He poured in wisdom.
I shall honor Her by listening as She speaks to me.
I shall implore Her to present Herself, reveal and invoke Herself in every aspect of my life.
When God created me, he poured Himself into me.
As I acknowledge myself as His creation, I honor God.
He dwells within me.

I am in you and you are in me. We are one. There can be no separation between us and God. There simply cannot be. He has created us from himself. We as joint heirs with Christ are in the Father.

Be.
I am.
Be.
I am.
Be.
I AM.
I am a part of the Great I AM.

Where is hell?—any place outside of the will of God. There we suffer from loneliness, disease, pain, hopelessness, despair, guilt, fear and the lack of the knowledge of who we are.

Seek to know who you are. Once the marvel of your creation as a handiwork of God is truly understood, you will immediately know to whom you belong. You can then take your place in the universe and fulfill the unfathomable potential that is you. You are uniquely important to the all of creation!

To be lead by God and to hear Him speak through the Spirit is the sweetest joy I know. To seek His holy will and to praise Him in spirit and truth is to build a holy refuse for my soul. To be directed to the vision and purpose of and for my life is to be assured the destination of heaven. To pursue heaven is to know that on this earth God will grant power to maintain the endeavor and peace that will abide throughout the pursuit. To commune with God is to allow release of earthly weights—guilt, sin, fear that fetter us and create barriers to God's gifts.

God is real. He does not change. He lives within me and is, therefore, always accessible to me. I live in Him. I am His; He is mine. He gives me power and strength as I am able to handle it.

Because God has invested Himself in me, there is nothing that I need to fear. God has supplied me with a light to see my way, wisdom to discern the truth and joy and peace to be content in this moment. I am blessed in deed.

I sought to teach, and I was taught.
I sought to give, and I was gifted.
I sought to lend comfort, and I was comforted.
I sought to give strength, and I was empowered.
I sought to praise God, and He blessed me.

There is within all of us the yearning to know who we are. Some part of us desires reconnection with the Creator. Our very souls long to reach up to God and know the fullness of being a part of the Great I Am. We long to BE.

God is the anchor of my soul, He holds me steady and true. Patiently He waits for my meanderings to cease. He waits for my vision to return. He waits lovingly for me to dock into eternity.

Lord, I seek to know your will and your way for my life. You know my hopes, dreams, challenges and issues. I quiet myself and seek to hear from you. I know you are the answer. Thank you.

The man who has understanding knows that this place is not his home. The physical trappings of the body and world cannot confine him to the small dimensions of this earthly habitat. The man of understanding has released his spirit and communes with God. In this divine association he finds peace and joy which span beyond the earthly realm into the dimension of timelessness where he is one with God. The divine association is the source of his excellent spirit. It is a spirit that he would not abandon for all of the world.

To live without God is the most frightening thing I can imagine. It is the very essence of an ever present hell.

Do we wait upon the Lord or does he wait on us? God knows

I Am Lifted

no time. He is always the same. He made provisions ready for us long before we were born. The storehouse of blessings to satisfy our needs has long been full. The key to open God's warehouse has been provided to us. Unfortunately, unlike God we exist in the illusion of time. We are a work in progress always developing, never finished while we continue to be subject to time's illusion. We labor to create our readiness to step into our blessings and acknowledge our purpose. Since there is no time with God, he knows that these things have already come to pass. It is we, who do not know.

Guilt, Anger and Fear

Sometimes we harbor within ourselves guilty secrets. To the extent that we shelter them, they control our lives. They constrain our joy and banish our peace. Yet, we cannot expose the painful "truth" because we fear that its exposure will precipitate loss within our lives. We fear loss of status, loss of relationship, loss of personal value. We delude ourselves into thinking that only by internalizing the pain can we maintain our freedom. We fail to realize that we are being held hostage by our emotional baggage. Freedom comes from allowing the light to shine within us. It is then that we can release the pain and find peace.

Today a young man showed me his bleeding hands and feet. He suffers from eczema. He told me that he thought his illness was a punishment from God, because He had not been in church for a while. He had a great deal of mental anguish. We explored his feelings as we talked more. He felt guilty for and ashamed of some of his behavior. I told him that God forgives our errors when we make them. We must forgive ourselves.

Many people suffer and cause themselves to be ill because they feel guilty, fearful and or ashamed. Those emotions alone cause or contribute greatly to illness. If they could forgive themselves, they would find that their burdens are lighter and illnesses healed.

Anger is one of the most destructive forces in the universe. It is a culmination of fear, guilt, rejection, confusion, misunderstanding and deceit all rolled into one. It has a life of its own and is directed by the physical mind as a tool of chaos and calamity. Anger gives birth to pain and illness. It estranges you from your brother by distorting your vision of him into something alien from yourself. Anger is caustic to everything it touches. It is not of God. When you attack your brother in anger, you attack yourself.

When you are in fear, go inside and ask the Holy Spirit to guide you. She will shine the light, and you will be able to see the truth of the matter. She will give you discernment so that you can find your way. She will give you understanding so that you will know that there is nothing to fear.

You must engage in the pursuit of a better life if you want it. The journey is not for the faint of heart. Nor is it for those who lack the discipline to seek and maintain the vision. The course is neither straight nor without regression. You will experience both brilliant dawns and midnights in the abyss. Maintain your journey.

Forgiveness

It is difficult for some of us to forgive because while we could not control the circumstance in which the pain was inflicted, we believe that we can control the breadth and depth of our resultant anger and its effects on others. We must learn that we cannot.

In surrender there is peace. Have you been hurt, misused, abused? Acknowledge your pain; know it for what it is. Do not resist it. For to resist it, is to perpetuate it and make it bigger. Embrace the pain as a reality and teaching tool of your life. Forgive your transgressor. By forgiving the offender, you sever him from you. Forgive yourself for being a victim. Through self-forgiveness, you unwrap the self-imposed mummy rags that bind the past so tightly to you. Each step toward total forgiveness advances you toward healing and peace. As you surrender the pain of yesterday, learn its lessons and forgive, you banish it forever.

I Am Lifted

In order to forgive, you must surrender resistance to the fact or condition. Acknowledge what is. Release the negativity and tension. This does not mean passive resignation, but active forgiveness and letting go. The time is always now.

Your ability to forgive speaks to your power to reclaim your future and live in the present.

Forgiveness is a miracle. Not only does forgiveness heal, it has the capacity to resurrect minds, bodies and souls. It releases both the giver and the receiver from a shared bondage. To forgive is to remove the blinds and allow the light of holiness to shine in our lives. The light banishes the shadows and exorcises our self-imposed demons lurking in them. The light of forgiveness has the power to allow those of us with heavy hearts or guilty minds to lift our heads. Once the demons have been banished and our heads have been lifted, we are free to unite with the Holy Spirit within us.

God stands forever ready to forgive us and recreate our lives. He shines the light upon us to enable us to discern our way to Him. If we quiet ourselves, we can hear His instructions as the Holy Spirit whispers them sweetly into our ears. If we open our eyes, we can see His plan unfold for us. When our purpose becomes His purpose, we become powerful beyond measure.

Our forgiveness is complete when we have forgiven ourselves. God forgave us our error during the moment it was committed. It is we who harbor the pain, guilt, shame and fear. When we release them, our eyes will open to the vision of the complete life that God has prepared for us.

Journey through Forgiveness

Today as I write, I find myself being challenged. How much of my life am I willing to disclose in order to share the lessons that I am learning in a way that demonstrates what I have hidden as the pain and shame of my life? Having emerged (or at least having thought I had emerged) from the pain that held me in captivity and the shame that shackled me to the past, I had no desire to revisit it and even much less desire to share it. But mine is a spiritual journey that I am compelled to share. I accept the teaching that where I am in my life is where I should be. There are lessons to be learned in this place. I further accept as the guiding principle of my life the fact that, "…all things work together for good for those who love God and are called according to his purpose." *(Romans 8:28)*. These thoughts give me courage and guide me toward disclosure.

One day while meditating, I saw my father. I reached out to him. He seemed angry with me. I was totally unsettled. I could not understand why he would be angry with me.

I Am Lifted

I spent a lot of time with my dad during his final illness. He and I had no issues to be discussed. I relished in the fact that he had been a good dad. He had given me the values of hard work, charity, focus and dedication to goals. I was well educated and a reasonably successful adult. I attributed these successes to him. So, as you would imagine, seeing him as angry was very perplexing to me. Yet, I could not shake it off.

I began to meditate on the issue. It soon became apparent to me that the anger I saw was mine. My father is dead and resting with God. He has no earthly emotion. The emotion was mine.

Once again I was perplexed. Why on earth would I be angry at my dad? I loved and admired him. He was my direct role model for so many things. I admired his faith and commitment to God. He was an avid reader who enthusiastically embraced politics. His advice was extraordinarily sound. My dad was tenacious in times of difficulty. He loved people and went out of his way to help those who needed help. A man of courage, he always stood up for his principles. He always did what he thought was right.

It was there that I realized the source of my anger. Sometimes what Dad thought was right was wrong.

I was born the last of nine children to loving parents. My siblings embraced me with enthusiasm. I was clearly well loved even though I suffered through being occasionally excluded by my brothers and reprimanded by my sisters. My childhood was magical. I romped around the farm, played hide and seek in the cornfields, fished in the creek and studied the ants and bugs under rocks. I was introduced to reading and quickly identified it as my first love. I believe each day at least one of my siblings tried to teach me something or help me understand that I was special. They taught me that

I was worthy of love. They also taught me how to look on the bright side of things. They praised me for my intellect and eagerness to learn. When I left my childhood, I believed I was strong, smart, happy, multi-talented and capable of accomplishing anything I wanted.

I did not see my father much during childhood. When I did see him, he was loving and kind toward me, but he gave my older sisters a hard time. He worked two and sometimes three jobs to provide for us.

My world changed at the dawn of my adolescence. My mom went to work, and Dad decided to change his work schedule to be at home with me after school. By that time, my sisters had all married and left home. I was left home, alone, with three brothers and Dad. I was immediately relegated to the status of domestic and cook.

One day I was a happy, self-confident kid; however, in a matter of months, I sunk into being a self-depreciating, insecure adolescent. I can mark the descent by the eruption of pimples and their resultant scars on my face. I was teased unmercifully and demeaned by my brothers. To make matters worse, my hair fell out. Then there was more teasing. "Your head looks like a basketball with a little bit of hair on it," one of my brothers teased me. On another occasion he talked to me about a girl at school who was popular and pretty. All the boys were falling over themselves to get to her. "She isn't pretty," my brother told me, "It's just that the rest of you girls are so ugly that you make her look good." My brothers did things to embarrass me in public places and in my home in front of their friends. I suffered through years of humiliation and mean teasing. There was even a period during which they hit me on the shoulder each time they passed me. But, the worse blows (literal) of my adolescence came from my father who had a penchant for whipping me with a belt or slapping me. My dad's decision to come home and be with me shuttered the doors and windows of my wonderful childhood and closeted me in a world of domination, abuse and dysfunction. On many occasions the love and acceptance that I felt from my father turned into acts of rejection, repression and recrimination.

The consistent message of my teen years was that every aspect of my life was contingent on my father's whim and mood. If he was happy, I was happy. If he was angry, I was sullen. Dad fussed. He was frustrated by many aspects of his life and he fussed loudly and often about them. One of his favorite sayings was, "You kids aren't worth the salt in your food." (Salt was very cheap in the latter sixties and early seventies, and I knew it.) Other times, as he pulled his belt from his pants, he would say, "I have a good mind to...." Whenever I heard those words, I knew that his mind was not good.

When my youngest brother had had enough of being whipped, he took a stick that Dad attempted to hit him with from Dad. My brother broke it across his knee. At that point, both Dad and I realized that I was the only target left. It was then that the facial slaps started coming more frequently.

Dad controlled the way I wore my hair—straight, no bangs. Any variance would precipitate at least one slap. He dictated the length of my skirts. "Don't wear that anymore," was a frequent refrain. I was not allowed to wear tights or white stockings. He monitored me so closely that he commented that something was 'wrong' with me on the morning of day that I started my first period.

I was not allowed to attend school games or parties. I was required to be home to wake him up for work. He worked midnights. I cooked and served him dinner and made his lunches. By the time I was fifteen, all my brothers had left home and I was alone with Dad. I was under his scrutiny almost constantly. When I was able to escape his gaze, I wore the mask of a happy, confident teen. I wore the mask to hide my cracked and diminished sense of self. I did not want to expose my shame.

At the age of nineteen, I received the last slap from my father. I think the facts that I had a job and was paying my own way through college gave me the courage to finally say to him, "No more." Unfortunately, it would not be the last time I felt myself to be abused.

Fast forward three years, I was a recent college grad and a newlywed. My life, by my estimation of things was clearly on track. I was married to a man whom I adored. There was nothing in the world more important to me than he was. I had begun my graduate studies and things were good. Yet, for some inexplicable reason, I felt uneasiness within me. One day when I was sitting alone on the couch looking at our beautiful wedding pictures, an awful sad feeling came over me. As my tears fell on the cellophane pages, I knew in that moment that the marriage would not last. Just then my husband came in the door. He saw me silently crying and asked the reason. As he took me into his arms, my muddled response was that I just loved him so much.

As the months went by, my quiet, lovingly passionate husband became angry, argumentative and dominating. One day we were arguing. He was upstairs and I was downstairs. He told me to come up to him. I refused. He came down, picked me up and took me upstairs so that we could argue in his venue. Although he did not hurt me physically, I later realized that the action marked the day that he began to take and I began to surrender what I believed to be my personal power. Once again, my self-esteem plummeted.

Time went on. As with most newlyweds, there were times when things were so sweet that they were nearly perfect. I believed in him. He was smart, articulate, handsome, funny

I Am Lifted

and during good times easy. One day he came home with a big beautiful plant for me. It had a tiny card that said simply, "------ loves Denise." I melted. I craved him. He was my delight. I did everything I could think of to make him happy. I later came to understand that I did far too much.

The parallels between my teen years and the circumstances of my first marriage were eerie. Both my dad and husband worked midnights. Both required the house to be silent and cold in order for them to sleep. Both were demanding and demeaning.

During the first nine months of our marriage my husband suffered a major disappointment. It seemed to devastate him. His outlook regarding many things changed. He became angry and argumentative. There was one particularly egregious, anger filled episode that marked the beginning of my living in almost constant fear. Once again I was in a relationship in which I had no power. Of course there were tears after the episode. Both of us cried. There were pleas of forgiveness that were granted and promises of changes. I told him that he had hurt my heart.

The hurtings escalated. He was more often angry than not. His anger was more like a rage that was directed toward me. I became virtually petrified by fear. I would not make even simple decisions without consulting him. I could not visit my family without his approval. Most times, he insisted that I wait until he could go along. I surrendered my friendships to avoid the anger. I modified the way I related to people. I was less friendly and particularly reserved in the company of males both adolescent and adult. Anything I did could precipitate recriminations. I surrendered and surrendered pieces of myself until I finally surrendered my light.

When things would get particularly bad for me, I would clean. I cleaned the kitchen, defrosted the freezer, cleaned the oven, mopped the floor and cleaned the bathroom. Cleaning was the only way I knew to numb the pain and reduce conflict.

There was no peace in our home. It was not a friendly place. Because my relatives found my home to be less than inviting, I had very few visitors. Once again I found myself isolated. Embarrassed and guilt ridden by what was happening, I could tell no one.

My family knew something was wrong. When my husband and I rented a garage apartment from my sister, she had the opportunity to experience my husband's rage first hand. She was frightened by it. She began to ask questions about the marriage.

My constant feelings of apprehension and discomfort began to take a toll on me. One day I realized that I could no longer think. My mind was befuddled and sounds of mental and spiritual confusion became deafening. Somehow through the haze I managed to realize that I would lose all of myself if things continued. Once again, I managed to say "No more." In three months we were divorced. It took another five-and-a-half years for the relationship to finally be over and another ten after that to totally surrender it.

During the first years following the divorce, we were able to discuss the issues of the marriage and resolve the anger.

As I revisited all of these issues, I discovered that my anger at Dad was not merely about what had happened in his home. It was more about that fact that his abuse made me accustomed to being a victim.

I discussed my father's actions with my mother while I was in the process of sorting out all of the memories of my teen years. She told me that he wanted so badly for his children to turn out well. He followed the only formula that he knew.

My mother apologized to me for her failure to protect me from my father's anger. I had never considered her to have any fault in the matter. I viewed her as I viewed myself—powerless.

My sister told me that she spoke with Dad while he was dying. She asked him why he had been so hard on us. He told her that he had done the best he could.

Nothing else could be required of him.

I have looked at it, railed against it, and questioned why I had to suffer the abuse. I now view it without passion or emotion. It is merely a collection of old shadows. I forgive all the actors including myself through the depths of my soul. I leave the shadows impotent and behind me.

What I learned:

When I surrendered, I surrendered not to the situation, but I surrendered my emotional attachment to the situation. I surrendered it to the Divine. At that point my peace was restored.

I have recently seen my father in meditation. He has offered me guidance which I have accepted.

Truth

Sometimes we choose not to see. We cling to our illusions and avoid the illumination of truth because we are afraid of making changes. We fear that we must give up something that we enjoy. We prefer to live in our creation of darkness.

Know the (your) truth and it shall set you free. *(John 8:32)*. How does one come into the knowledge of his or her truth? Does it show up, reveal itself and say, "This one is for you?" Is there a sage who passes along your way to enlighten you? Or, perhaps, there is an angel who gently waves her wings over you to bring you into a state of revelation of your truth. Or maybe there are time-sensitive crystals that have been peppered into your consciousness that, at the appointed time, reveal bits and pieces of your individual truth—the who you are and the why you are. The purpose that you were created to serve is contained within your truth.

There is something that rises up within each of us to present and confirm our truth. The ignition of purposeful passion is the canvas that will reveal your truth. The work applied in furtherance of passion is the paint brush that displays the brilliance of your truth or divinity to the world on the canvas. For, your truth reflects the light that God placed within you.

Meditate on your truth for it is not small. It is powerful and broadly significant. Its breath will touch those you will never know, but their lives will be enlightened and enriched by the recognition of the freedom and advantage your truth has given you. Your light will lighten the path of others.

Seek to know your truth. Listen to the voice inside you. Do you yearn for more? Do you have the feeling that you are not quite there? Is there something unfinished? Have you envisioned bits and pieces of another more abundant life that you feel is yours? Does it excite you? Empower and embolden yourself to dream your biggest dream. Dream, dream in bold color with vivid details. Where do you want to be? What do you want to do? How do you plan to serve humanity? Are you excited? Write the vision—write it! Ask the Divine for what you want. Listen as She tells you how to get it. Proceed in the light of the freedom of your truth. You are incomparable!

If you lack joy, attend to the needs of others. The display of love will renew your wellspring of joy. If you lack peace, dissociate yourself from the materialism of the world. Instead focus on the bounty of God. In your meditations peace will be found. If you lack love, open your heart and arms to God who has been waiting for your readiness to receive him.

Life is Just a Dream—Illusion

Imagine that you uncovered evidence that your life is not real. It is, in fact, a figment of your imagination. Your body is a mental creation designed to house your guilt caused by a breach from creation. You strayed from the truth. In order to validate yourself, you dreamed a world that revolved around you. In your dream, you bestowed upon your body senses: sight, hearing, touch, taste, and smell. You created certain rules for the governance of your body. You determined those things which cause pleasure and those that cause pain. You went so far as to define bad pleasure and good pain. While you created your body to define yourself, you, by stuffing your soul into it, disassociated yourself from the power of your soul. You totally alienated the Holy Spirit. You created a disconnect between yourself and your Creator.

You have no body—no hands, no legs, no lips, no feet, no mouth. The things that you think are all borne of illusion. In other words, you do nothing. You don't love. You don't hate. You don't work—itch, sleep, dream, have relatives, and you were not born. You do nothing. You have no life as

I Am Lifted

you think you know it—it is all your mental creation that is nothing.

Now you awaken to..........

Are we so strong that we can change or pervert God's creation? Our view of ourselves as filthy rags is a mental perversion based on illusion. As a consequence it is not real. God is real. Anything that He created is real. Anything that is not created of him is not real. Your assessment of who you are if it is anything less than perfect, full, loved, blessed, peaceful and joyous is self-depreciating and is illusory. God created you perfectly as a reflection of Himself. He does not change. As a part of Him, you do not change. Your mind is far too impotent to alter God and his creation. –Go to Him and discover who you are.

You can never be satisfied outside of yourself. Your pursuit of things, titles, people and relationships will never be fully realized because you are not satisfied with yourself. You always long for something more.

I spoke with a self-made, wealthy man. He described to me how close he and his wife were in the early days of building their business. Their single purpose and vision had a binding effect on their relationship. As the money came, they drifted farther and farther apart. Her ravenous desire for the acquisition of things caused him to work harder and harder. His fear of losing what he had built forced him to work longer and longer hours and more and more days. The complaint from his spouse that he never spent time with the family and its ensuing arguments began to rip the fabric of the relationship.

He and I were together to discuss his son who was skipping school and abusing substances. As he mourned over the destructive path his son seemed to be taking, he was reflective regarding his own path. He surmised that his wealth had taken on a life of its own. People viewed him differently, and he projected a view of himself which had to do with superiority, power, privilege and right. These notions were unintentionally, or perhaps intentionally, passed down to his children. Yet, he maintained the underlying paranoia of losing it all. The man confessed to me that a life based on the pursuit of wealth was no life at all. He was committed to changing his life because he wanted something—something more.

I believe the something more he needed was the truth of who he was. The answers that he sought and the ones that all of us seek are within us. Look inward to discover that you are a creation of God. You were created as a soul long ago and have always resided in God. In the realm of the Spirit, you are whole, complete and lack nothing. As a creation of God, you are a part of him. It is Him to whom you belong. This knowledge is the only true satisfaction you will ever know. For it is truth. Other people or things cannot satisfy you any more than you can satisfy yourself. Satisfaction, otherwise known as salvation, is of God.

To see this world and to know that it is an illusion is a great blessing. It lets us know that there is no need to worry.

Your world is a figment of your imagination. It is something you conjured up in order to confuse yourself and maintain separation from God. Your body is under the control of your mind. Your mental state can cause healing or destruction to it. Your sleeping eyes behold nightmarish images of hate, greed, fear, guilt and pain that were created by you, for you. Release your mind; disavow the rantings of your imagination. Return to your spiritual self and reclaim your place with God.

Life as God created it wants for nothing. Life, as man has conjured it, is never satisfied and wants for everything except for what it has, the present moment. We spend so much time investing in our self-created world by acquiring things such as money, land, houses, titles and other status symbols that we lose sight of our God created spiritual life. It is for that reason that we constantly seek bigger and better. Yet, if we turn inward to the holy altar within us, we will feel the joy and contentment of being complete. We will need no more.

When we feel adrift, we must reach out to God. We must avail ourselves to the hands at the helm. He has already plotted the course. Once we surrender our fear, we will know that we were never really adrift but deluded by fear into thinking so.

Do not place more value on this life than it deserves. This world is not your home. To value things that are in it is to invest in shadows. When the light comes fully into your life, the shadows will dissipate.

Peel the self that you have created away from your true self and behold the perfect creation of God.

If there is something over which you can claim exclusive ownership, you can rest assured its ownership will not secure your place in eternity.

Service

Men are stewards with regard to their talents, time, money, physical, mental abilities. They are stewards with regard to their resources and privileges—each privilege is a sacred talent to be used toward spiritual goals. People are responsible for not only what they do but for what they are capable of doing. Whatever we hold in trust for God, we must use for His increase.

How would your life be different if you understood that everything you possess did not belong to you but to God? Would you conduct your life differently if you understood that you had to render an account of every talent, every possession, every relationship that you owned or in which you were involved? Would your life be more purposeful and more fulfilled?

We are stewards of the Earth. Yet, we rob her of the wisdom of her creation.

Salvation

Salvation belongs not to you, but is your gift to share as a means of drawing others to the light. Your salvation is a sacred gift over which you must exercise stewardship. It is the responsibility of everyone who has received the divine gift to offer it to others. The offer is made continuously through day-to-day ministrations. The offers of kindness, the glow of peace and joy, the demonstrations of discernment are all calls to share in the gift of salvation. Salvation is a beaconing light to others to share the goodness of God.

Sin and guilt are not the guiding principles of my relationship with God. Joy, peace and grace are the gifts of my affiliation with His goodness.

What does Jesus mean when he commands us to deny ourselves? He is telling us to release the idols of this world that direct and govern our actions. The self-image that directs us to act a certain way, the social position that supports or depresses our self-image are both idols that dictate much of our lives. Christ admonished us to abandon these things because they have no spiritual value. Mere illusions, they cannot transcend from this world to the next. These idols will evaporate just as our last earthly breath vanishes.

In denying ourselves, we elevate our vision to God and His plan of salvation for us. We relinquish the things of this world and press, "…toward the mark for the prize of the high calling of God in Jesus Christ." *(Philippians 3:14).* This is the prize that will take us from earth to Heaven. It will lose nothing in translation from this life to the next. Praise God.

Why does the Shepherd leave the ninety and nine to find the one lost sheep? *(Luke 15:4)* It is the will of God that none be lost. Every soul must be won. In Jesus' prayer in the garden, He gave God a report of those entrusted to him. *John 17:12* "Those that thou gavest me I have kept, and none of them is lost, but the son of perdition; that the scripture might be fulfilled."

Being engrafted into our brother through Christ and entwined with our brother through the Holy Spirit, each of us has a part in the salvation of the other. We are all bound by love to work diligently in the vineyard to assure that every soul is reconciled back to God.

Pain

Pain is often solicited. Our actions and thoughts often call out for the visitation of pain. The quests for those things which are not spiritual press hard upon our earthly vessels. We work too hard; we do not work enough. We play too hard; we do not play hard enough. Our lives are characterized by imbalance. We concentrate on things that have no real value, no place in the eternal scheme of things. We compromise our mental and physical health in the pursuit of idols. We convict ourselves with judgment, guilt and shame. We are stressed out, strung out and played out. We suffer the pain that we have invited into our lives.

When you are in pain, seek to know the true source of it. It is very seldom what you think it is. Seek to know the lesson being taught. What is there within you that you have ignored that needs to be practiced in your daily life? Do you need to acknowledge your state of wholeness? Are you walking in the power that God gave you? Have you visited your well-spring of joy, the Holy Spirit? The issue is not what you think it is. Dig deeper.

Surrender

I surrender my life, my love, my thoughts, my relationships, my ambitions, my self-concepts, my possessions, my perceptions, my concepts, my guilt, my fear, my hatefulness, my judgments, my blindness, my inconstancy, my willfulness, my determinations and my selfishness to God. Make of me what you will and use me in your way.

Last night I grappled with an intense family issue. It was not so much that I was mad. I was more upset at what I perceived to be an attempt at disempowerment. Through my meditation I came to know that my power comes from God. I cannot be stripped of it. Power was not the issue. It was then that I moved to acceptance. I surrendered my resistance to the situation and accepted it as it was. The tension evaporated. My peace was restored, and the solutions became clear.

I Am Lifted

The other day I awoke at peace. I felt as though I had come into myself—calm and peaceful. Despite a frenetic morning or trying to remember everything, pack the car and get on the road, I was at peace. My husband and I started out on a three hundred and fifty mile road trip to Tahquamenon Falls. As we drove along, we munched trail mix (which I should not eat), chatted, I studied the maps and read about interesting places. We stopped at a rest stop. I went in and placed my purse carefully within the handicapped stall. Minutes later we were on the road. I slept for at least an hour. When I woke up we had a retirement discussion. Those never go well for us. That time, however, we managed to put all of the issues on the table and leave them there for later discussion. We continued contentedly on our journey. A few moments later my husband pointed to the Mackinaw Bridge. I excitedly reached for my phone to send the kids a picture of it. My excitement melted as I searched the car and came to the sad conclusion that I had left my purse at the rest stop. We immediately left the highway and turned back south. As my husband drove, we tried to identify where we had stopped. We identified an area north of Saginaw. By my calculations, we had travelled one hundred and thirty miles from the stop. It would take a good two hours and then some to get back to it—that is if it was still there. I called the kids with my husband's phone and asked them not to call my phone; I did not want to draw attention the purse. I called the Michigan State Police. After reaching several different posts, a wonderful dispatcher, Toni, told me that she would send a car out to check and see if the purse was at the identified stop.

Meanwhile my daughter called me back. I told her if it was gone, it was just gone. It had money, credit cards and other personal items. They were all replaceable. I told her that on the large scale of things, if losing my purse was the worst thing to happen to me I was truly blessed. Its loss would represent a minor inconvenience. I was at peace with it.

The police officer called me back and told me that the purse was not there. She also told me that there were no stationary employees at the rest stops. They went from stop to stop cleaning. I told my husband that I wanted to go back anyway.

As we continued our retrogression, we passed the rest area that we identified to the police and realized that it was not the correct stop. We continued on to the next stop. Once we arrived, I checked the restroom area. No purse. I went to a side door which was open. There was no one there, but music was playing in a little office. I went throughout the station looking for the employee—no luck. I told my husband that I believed there was someone working at the station. He pointed to someone on the far side of the grounds picking up trash. We walked over to him. My husband asked if he worked there. He nodded. "I left my purse here about four hours ago."

"What's your name?" he asked. After I identified myself, he said, "I have it." We all broke out in excited celebration—all three of us were hugging each other.

It was a happy reunion. Nothing was disturbed in my purse. I tried to give Bob a finder's fee. He would not accept it.

The celebration of all of this is not just the fact that my purse was given back to me in the condition which I left it, but more importantly, I was able to perceive the loss as what is was, and establish peace. I did not worry at all. I surrendered it.

I am growing.

I Am Lifted

How is it that we are strengthened through surrender? When we surrender to God, we acknowledge that God is all there is. We understand that there is nothing else. If there is nothing outside of God, then all is within God. By surrendering ourselves to God, we envision ourselves as a part of God impotent and hopeless without Him. We also realize that in Him, we are powerful beyond measure with Him.

So often in life we surrender to the wrong things. We surrender to people who would dominate us, to habits, eating disorders or drugs. But, when it comes to the time to surrender to the Creator, we resist. The sweetest surrender is to the Divine. When we realize that we alone have no power over the situation, that we cannot heal our pain, we should surrender it to the Divine and trust that She has worked it out. We need only relax and make ourselves ready for the revelation.

If queried, most of us would readily admit that we want God in our lives. More than that, many of us would say that we want God to direct our lives. We know, at least cerebrally, that if God is in control that everything will be "all good" or greater. Yet there are those places in our lives in which we close the door to God. Those are the rooms that house our dirty little secrets and pain. Behavior that we know to be out of alignment with God is kept in the room. Pain that we suffered at the hands of others that we are unwilling to share because it may lower the esteem that others have for us is kept in the room. We keep our lusts, jealousies, hatreds, guilt and fear in the room. The room is guarded by our minds as though it is filled with precious jewels. That past hurt that we keep reliving, that indignity that we cannot forgive, those insecurities based on relationships—all of that junk is in the room.

We must acknowledge the contents of the room. God knows what is there. To the extent that we relish in these tortures, we deny the Holy Spirit access and preclude Her from ministering to us to resolve the issues. We must open the door and allow Her light to enter in. We will then see and feel each torture dissipate. For in the light, all illusion fades away.

Blessings

When we say that we are waiting for our blessings, we ignore the fact that everything that God has for you has already been provided. We need to embrace it now. We don't have to wait for God to show up. He is here. Likewise, we don't have to wait for His miracles. They are here. They become ours when we exhibit the faith to embrace them. The Great I AM is ever present and always ready to bless us.

Faith

The place where you are is the place where you need to be to vault yourself onto the next level. There are lessons to be learned in this space. The lessons learned will unleash your feet and provide you with the power to move on. What then is the lesson? While there is no easy answer, I can assure you that the fruits of the Holy Spirit are involved. Do you need to buttress your faith so that you can actually believe that not only is God able to provide, but that His word is true? Perhaps you need to develop kindness and patience. Are you lacking in love or the ability to see your brother as yourself? Do you lack humility? Are you given to despair? Do you feel as though you have lost your way or perhaps there is no way? Renew your connection and strengthen your faith. Your immobility and spiritual discomfort is a signal that there is some sort of disconnect, a failure in your faith or your relationship with God. Seek to know the cause. Seek revelation through prayer, meditation and communion with God. Learn the cause. Learn the lesson. Overcome the fear and you will quickly find yourself at the next level.

Peter asked Jesus to bid him to come to him. Because of Peter's belief in Christ, he was able to walk on water. *(Matthew 14:28).*

I too believe in the power of Christ. Because I am a joint-heir with Christ, I believe that the gifts God gave him are also mine. My gifts, or the activation of them, are based on the same contingency as Christ's. The power comes from God. So, as long as I live and serve totally in His purpose, I may utilize my gifts. I can have no doubt, no fear, no guilt and no animosity. I must be at one with the purpose of my creation. At that point, I too will be able to walk on water.

Faith precipitates blessings in people's lives.

When I was a little girl, my father's place of employment closed and he joined the ranks of the unemployed. He diligently sought work, but in time, he saw his savings dwindle down to nothing. He decided that he wanted to work for one of the auto companies. Each day for a month, he went to the personnel office. He went so many times that the personnel manager would greet him with the phrase, "No work today Eaddy." Yet, my father persisted in going. On the morning that my dad knew would be the final day of going to the office, the manager started the familiar refrain, "No work to—"

My dad interrupted him saying, "Yes, there is work today. I have nine children at home and only five dollars in my pocket." Dad was right. That was the day he was hired. He secured a good wage, health benefits and the beginning of prosperity for our family.

Faith transforms visions into reality.

I attended a professional development conference in Chicago. I rarely eat breakfast when I stay at hotels because I prefer to sleep until the last moment. (My world is one of continuous sleep deprivation.) One morning I broke my routine and went down to breakfast. A beautiful little girl about two years old was sitting at the table beside me. Looking at her simply made me happy. She was dressed in bright colors and had matching barrettes in her hair. "You are so beautiful," I told her. "Where did your mommy get a little girl so beautiful?"

Her mother looked at me and smiled. "There is a story to that. Would you like to hear it?" she asked.

"Of course."

She told me that for many years, she and her husband had tried to have a baby. They underwent testing and found that there were too many problems. They were told they would never have children. For awhile, they went about life trying to accept the fact that they would be childless. Then one day a "feeling" came over her, and she knew that she would become a mother. Everyday, starting that day, she wrote a prayer and put it into a shoebox. Her husband, a mail carrier, watched her deposit her prayer into the box each morning before he went to work. One day he came home early. He was so excited that he could not contain himself. He asked her to guess what he had found on his route that day. She said that she had no idea what he was talking about, and she wasn't in the mood for guessing games. He was persistent. He went into the bedroom and came out with her shoebox. She asked him if he had found a shoebox full of prayers. He shook his head at her and told her no. Then he told her that he had found a shoebox full of answers. She still did not understand. With a broad smile

I Am Lifted

across his face, he explained that he had found a shoebox with a baby in it.

As my jaw dropped, she looked at me and said, "This is that baby."

What We Learn from Children

Children provide wonderful examples for us. A child longs to hear the voice of her mother. She is never as comfortable or secure as when she rests in the arms of a loving parent. Children search to know their parents' faces and respond positively to their loving attention. Jesus admonished us that we must come as a child. *(Matthew 18:3).*

Have you ever had a lackluster day when you somehow managed to go into the presence of a happy, smiling, young child? Didn't your heart open to embrace the joy? And, before you knew it, there was a smile on your lips. What you experienced was a purely spiritual connection. The spirit of the child reached out to you. Your spirit responded, easily without any effort or cognition. That is how the Holy Spirit connects with us-- easily, effortlessly, without motive or thought. You were able to connect with the child because your spirit recognized itself in the child. You remembered that in your state of creation, you were one and the same.

When small children see other small children, they are delighted. They embrace. Seeing their image in the other, they call each other 'baby' thereby signifying their love and oneness. We would do well to learn the lessons that babies can teach us.

When my daughter was three years old, she asked me for a brother or a sister. I told her that her dad and I were very happy with the one, little, special girl that God had given us. We were not having anymore children. Not satisfied with that answer, she consulted with her dad. She made the same request for a brother or sister. Again, she was told that we were not having anymore children. She came back to me very unhappy with the both of us. She told me that she knew whom to ask. She would ask God.

Each night for about four months when she said her bedtime prayers, she asked for a brother or a sister. Then one night she stopped. I was relieved because I thought she had forgotten about it. Two weeks later, I learned why she had stopped praying. Her prayer had been answered. I was pregnant.

I thank God for her wisdom, faith and persistence. Her faith brought her brother, a true sunshine and light child, into our lives. We would not be complete without him!

Change

We often respond to change with fear, diffidence, discomfort and anxiety. Those emotions are stimulated by our failure to focus on the moment. Once we are able to focus on the moment, we will be able to shine the light of truth on the issues. The first truth is that there are no mistakes. We are in our present moment for it to lend instruction which propels us closer to perfection. The second truth is that in this moment everything we need has been provided. I know this because we are here and within us are all the resources we need. The third truth is that the Holy Spirit stands ever-ready to minister to us, to shed light and help us discern our way. The final truth is that change is an illusion of our minds that we will come to understand.

If we could realize that spiritually we are changeless and safely resting in God, we could more readily dance the dance of change in this world without fear. It is, after all, an illusion.

Be

Be like the lily: do not toil, do not stress. *(Matthew 6:28-29)*. Just BE. Let yourself evolve into the fullness of His creation. Know fully that you cannot make anything of yourself. That which was created whole does not need your interpretation or embellishment. Simply BE. Your alignment with God will call forth all the gifts invested in you and cause fruit to burst forth.

Freedom is in God. It is the right to BE. In that way you are free to unfold your true self. If you are consciously aware that you are in God and God is in you, you are free. In your freedom you have boundless access to the gifts of the universe. You are joy, light, purpose, peace and love. These gifts radiate as the essence of you. Your freedom craves the completeness of Being—BEing in God. You will not wander.

I recently invited a young friend of mine to speak at my Wednesday youth seminar at my church. He had been incarcerated for three years. One of the first things he told my youth was that they should just Be. "Know who you are and be yourselves," he told them. "The rest of the stuff that happens is not important."

I asked him how he had come into this knowledge. He explained that he had been in the 'hole' or solitary confinement for eighty days while he was in prison. It was pitch-black. He could not see his hand in front of his face. There was nothing to do but to surrender. He recognized where he was, why he was there, and he stopped fighting against it. It was when he gained acceptance that he began the journey into himself. It was through that journey that he found the freedom to BE. He came to understand that all the confusion, game playing, braggadocio and criminal actions were a part of his life of delusion. None of it contained any truth. As a consequence, none of it was real. He recognized the fact that in order for actions to be purposeful and real, they must serve others in ways that will enhance their lives.

My friend now feels a responsibility to reach out to youth and help them avoid the mistakes he made. He understands himself now. He is a part of something bigger, something better, something Divine.

I am happy to report that he is working and is a junior, majoring in engineering at a prominent university.

Show up for your life.
Be present in your life.
Take charge of your thinking.
Take charge of your doing by surrendering yourself.
Align yourself with the will of God.
Recognize who is in control.
Spice up your life.
Season it with loving.

I Am Lifted

Clean out your emotional closets.
Throw out
    Guilt,
    Shame,
    Envy,
    Grudges,
    Evil thinking and
    Bad habits.
Draw closer to God.
Celebrate yourself as a part of God and your life.
You are a wonderful creation.

We spend so much of our time thinking that we do not allow ourselves to unfold as God has created us.
In those times, I think becomes the nemesis of I am.

Time

In the *Book of Thomas 91:2* Jesus said, "You examine the face of heaven and earth, but you have not come to know the one who is in your presence, and you do not know how to examine the present moment." We spend so much of our time bemoaning the past and anticipating the future that we neglect the only reality that is ours: Now. The past has gone and escaped our grasp. The future is a vapor of our imagination. Now is ours to celebrate. Now is ours to embrace. Whatever this present moment presents to us, we should rejoice and celebrate its potential to teach, inform and enrich our lives. It is all we have. It all we will ever have.

In time, my vision will become clear and I shall behold the reality of God in my life. In time my hearing will become acute and I shall always hear his voice. In time my spirit shall soar and transcend the troubles and limits of this world. In

I Am Lifted

time my spirit shall make the leap from time to eternity. Time will be no more.

Time is made for man's perfection. It allows us an opportunity to come to re-know God. It creates circumstances under which we learn the character of God. Time lends itself to events that demonstrate to us that God is not separate from us. It also teaches us that we are not separate from our brothers. When we truly begin to learn and appreciate the fact that God is in us as well as every living thing, we realize that we are a part of the great tapestry of life. At the point that we all know that we and God are one, time will roll up and be no more.

Affirmations

God is within me.
There He waits
ready to reveal
to me the greatness
that was always my own.

I am an expression
of God's love for the world.

My life was not meant for me.
It is God's gift to others.
It is meant to exalt, encourage,
enlighten, protect and serve and defend.

I was born for purpose which was ordained
before my conception. *(Ephesians 2:10)*.

I Am Lifted

When I serve my purpose,
my life is filled with abundance
and my song is praise.
When I fail to serve my purpose,
I am in need and want.
My song is silenced.

I am connected to all points of the universe.
If I am out of purpose, the universe is diminished.
God seeks to have the universe restored at all times.

If I am out of purpose,
I am out of communication with God.
Lord, please lead me to my purpose.

God is speaking.
He continuously speaks to me.
If I listen, I can hear Him.
He tells me that all I need,
I have.
My every present moment
has been provided for.
I need only to hear Him reveal His plan.
He has considered every contingency.

If I feel powerless, God has power for me.
If I feel sick, He has well-being for me.
If I feel unworthy,
He lets me know that I am highly favored.
Because God loves me fiercely,
He has poured himself into me.

I am powered by God.
I am a reflection of God.
I am awesome!

Resist engaging the forces that would bring disharmony into your life. Do not be lured by the enticement to respond measure for measure. Speak peace to the situation instead. Cover the usurper of peace with the blanket of forgiveness.

Everything my mind tells me is not real. Nothing my mind tells me is real. I will seek to know the truth of the matter.

Oh how sweet the joy that dwells within the wonderful affiliation with God!

Breathe!

I will take a moment today and allow myself to rise above thought and enter the place of joy and peace.

I will reflect on the beauty and
meditate on the goodness of God.

Learning the words of faith and association
with God is easy.
Conforming my conduct to demonstrate
their truth is the greater challenge.

Today I will spend time exploring and
celebrating the Divine potential of
each moment.

Test of reality: if it is eternal, it is real.
If it exists only in time; it is not.

I will look inside myself to discover the portion of
the destiny of the universe that lies within me.

I will seek to know the truth, understand and forgive.

I will be. I will be guided by life.
I won't direct life.
I will let life direct me.

I will create space in my life for
love,

forgiveness,
peace and
joy.

Do not strive for happiness.
Know that God created you whole, without lack.
Simply BE happy.
It is your normal state in creation.

I see and feel God working in my life.
I will listen for His instruction and cling to His word.
I will do His will with enthusiasm.

Charity shines the light
of love and truth
through which men are saved.

I will bathe the feet of Jesus
with the tears of my sorrows
as I surrender
my cares and myself to Him.

Lord, let not my self created illusions
dominate my thoughts. Please transform my thoughts of
want to reflections of plenty.
Restructure my thoughts
from chaos to meditations of
order and peace.
Direct my thoughts away from pain and
reconfigure my heart and mind
to embrace ease and wellness.
Cease my mindless meanderings and

I Am Lifted

focus my thoughts on your will
and the perfection you have created
for my life.
Renew me into right relationship
with you.
Remove the mask from my
life so that I may dwell
in joy with you.

My Spiritual Objectives

To see God in everyone
To see without judgment
To view the world with compassion
To know myself as a child of God
To surrender, completely
To worship in spirit and in truth.

This journey has been particularly wonderful for me. Each step of the way I have been lifted. I have been able to explore the old pains of adolescence, divorce and my mistakes. I confronted many of my issues, acknowledged the reality of their existence as I viewed them without emotional attachment; I placed them into the hands of the Divine and moved beyond them.

As I come to the end of these pages, I celebrate my

I Am Lifted

personal growth and the exciting potential it holds for me to help others live their greatest lives. I have been spiritually enriched and immensely blessed. When I consider the title I Am Lifted, I realize that it has not so much to do with me as it has to do with the great I AM, the creator of the universe. Each time I am able to see myself more clearly, understand whose I am, the great I AM is lifted. Being a part of God, and God being a part of me, we enjoy a great symbiosis whenever I am aligned with his will for me. As I serve my purpose, I reach out to my fellow man in celebration of our creator. Doing this lifts both God and me. God is the light within me. As I shine my light I am (the little) and I AM the everything is lifted.

Come and exalt the Lord with me.

Denise Eaddy-Richardson

Denise Eaddy-Richardson is a teacher, an attorney and a counselor who has recently founded the company Passion for Purpose and embarked upon a career of motivational speaking and life coaching. An engaging personality, Denise is able to captivate and inspire members of all age groups in multiple venues including lectures, workshops, personal counseling and coaching sessions. The single objective of all of her work has been and continues to be empowerment of those with whom she works. Her approach to her work as well as her life is spiritual.

LaVergne, TN USA
25 March 2011
221680LV00001B/69/P